PAINTING

Stephen Ratcliffe

chax 2014

Some of these poems have appeared in *Bombay Gin, Kenning, Syllogism, Tinfish,* and *Van Gogh's Ear.*

Cover image: Oona Ratcliffe, *Yellow Beach*, 1998.
Oil on Canvas, 19 1/8 x 10 3/4 inches. Private Collection.

ISBN 978-0-9894316-5-1

Chax Press
411 N Seventh Ave Ste 103
Tucson Arizona 85705-8388
USA

For Oona and Johnny

"I paint the view from my window; one particular spot, determined by its position
in the architecture of a house, I paint ochre."

— Ludwig Wittgenstein, *Remarks on Colour* (10e)

"In visual perception a color is almost never seen as it really is
-- as it physically is."

— Josef Albers, *Interaction of Color* (1)

color of painting reflecting what's seen when he turns back, starts to see buildings on a hill
(sound) in morning light, how the woman's legs intersect the man sleeping in a dream (syllables)
for example the family on a sidewalk, child who takes her father's hand half in hers, after that

second bird landing on branch followed by motion of mass and weight, the position of the observer
who sits in a car in the parking lot (waves) no one sees, voice of the person behind the camera
hand held, another in the car that spins out of control, which house pictured on which screen

where the man sleeps determined by logistics of place, location in that sense analogous to car's
trajectory throwing off sparks as it swerves (left) across the center divide, how the child looked
filmed in action the man behind the wheel hasn't planned on, each word like a form of possible color

2

bottle of iris on a counter, person who wakes up when the girl walks in at 2:30, climbs into bed next to her mother, whose position shifts away from him, legs pulled toward other (breath) side, eye (closed) approximately green though she says she doesn't notice, counting a number of days

look of lights through the bedroom window after he wakes in the dark, doesn't go back to sleep thinking of how what hasn't happened won't be understood, motion defined as the weight of bread on the man's tongue falling into a dream in which the picture frame is shattered, buried in sand

how the child will be given directions to the house she hasn't ever seen before, from whose window (lights) the city is visible in a painting the color of which can only be imagined, said painting the actual size of a landscape looking out on it (present) that moment, registered as he recalls breast of robin on bare branch of tree (plum) identified by its color in relation to all known instances of that, terms like "red," "red orange" and "orange" being approximate (parenthesis) given that the viewer hasn't moved, lens of glasses as they fall to the concrete thus broken

arrangement of color in a system of painting, the mother next to her son on the opposite side of the table across from whom the man will be sitting beside the child who becomes his thought (that) spectrum of pigments seen in a relation between blue triangles in the upper right corner

thought after thought, the girl who answers it as she walks out the front door meaning to be like that woman, lipstick (red), eyes white, her figure fuller as the grey car pulled away like space after painting it, which isn't the same as dark green of background extending beyond the window grey tape on the car door (blue) peeling, as weather changes or the street (closed) filled with sand

has fallen, a girl leaving the house in the dark a perception of body the closer it comes to physical

plane of action, rhythm of two scenes in which sexual contact happens offstage (implied) in words only

idea or shape of the body clothed in space approximate to piano the figure plays, present as acoustic

phenomena in the distance (note) a glass plane reflects, as plane overhead or siren from the freeway

implicit in change as a form of life, tulips at the end of a performance (yellow) dancers will hold

as recollection, hypothesis based on his belief that the ring (missing) means something, perception

of events fallen out of order (chaos) implying the blue car is older than she thinks, color of petal

(vase) the same as ground but lighter, the child who paints it falling into her arms instead of a car

woman in jacket (blue) silk across a crowded room, shoulders and faces leaving the table where drinks
are being poured, others wanting to be seen in public (dancing) instead of the stage upon which men
in suits move in formal lines (geometry), women in black (stretch) turn prior to motion of a hand

how instead of falling asleep, after the car unable to park (crowd) across the street turns right,
she leaves herself open to the potential of gravity, weight (man's) fallen as if from the branches
whose buds (pink) are about to unfold, speaking now of the baby in the next frame beginning to suck

history unfolded at the corner (car) the man transcribes after thinking it, which isn't what happened
but changed (interpretation) in retrospect, the dancer's gesture as she cradles his face in her palm
(cupped) moving from stage right with arms like a swan's wings, one hand in the other's description

said of sound, the man returning to the green of grass coming up, small orange flowers in a clump, wind from northwest (abstract) continuous as time (momentum) or the sound of men digging up a road, scraping dirt from culvert at the end of winter, the feeling of air in the house having been closed

or say that the woman wakes up, having slept for hours in the middle of the day in an upstairs room (etching), the man next to the telephone when it rings a part of memory selected as if by accident, like perception of skin tone after months without sunlight, as light itself will begin to be felt

which isn't the same as waking in the dark, body in proximity to its dream of landscape in act one, quick bright things come to confusion (green) pulling the grass from the lavender, Belle of Portugal thus beginning to fall the longer its tendrils (rose) extend into space, in the next series of moments

fog moving in after sunrise, sound of birds (unseen) in the field across the fence beyond which more
distant sounds of water (swell) 10 feet on the radio, arrangement of poppies (red) on a blue violet
background whose rhythms interpret space in terms of the woman's relation to a man, moving forward

facing the couch, shirt above a bare leg (pose) recorded in the mind's eye at 24 frames per second,
first person (man) turned toward back of woman's head which is leaning (sideways) above his stomach,
water in bath less than warm in that experience of the house she will begin to imagine calling "home"

driving toward it, image projected in the rhythm of its colors in two or three dimensions (landscape),
words minus actions (missing) making that event more than present, as if memory itself could bring
something back, nothing to be concealed at this point given flexibility of green and blue motion

8

walking out the door, woman leaving her jacket (black) on the back of the chair by the other door
who phones to say it wasn't a mistake to have left it, sounds of two voices in the hall (proportion)
as a car moves into the oval (asphalt) in front of a building whose stairs may be climbed to the next

arrangement on a table, two bowls divided by a pear-shaped something (blue) moments after an explosion
the man perceives as a beautiful (acoustic) object, color saturated as words on the page the audience
listed under names of the actors at the start of the play, which brings up the experience of what is

said of color, perception of the owl (unseen) that flies in the night heard as the angle of paper's
surfaces, the woman walking in a line of women who gets up to walk the still dark streets, landscape
of bottles whose scale of tones (mute) defines the space filled when one person moves next to another

9

bodies in close proximity (foreground) turning over to the opposite side, her head on his shoulder
registered as touch (unconscious) he doesn't seem to notice, something about the color of the books
on the shelf translated to wind in the highest branches (bending) against the blue sky, whose leaves

mean to be present, this phenomenon transcribed the moment it happens, which is why the film records
the man falling asleep in his chair (action) offstage, who remembers it as perception the ear hears,
eye imagines (visual) as space divided into triangles on the left, the nearly perfect purple wedge

lower right hand corner, abstract in the sense that a sound becomes the relation between first person
and second, two green eyes focused in two blue (itself) reflections, weight of water when it pushes
forward at the end of the line's shore large enough to break bone, glass, the swimmer floating in

runs over log (submerged) in the break, sea calm except for that obstruction, as the person who builds
fires for warmth in the morning or wants to go out (waves) when it isn't blue, not clear but no wind
in the white (lower) sky before it rains, which hasn't happened in the left corner, out the window

tobacco plants (missing) dragged across a fence, the person who appears at the edge of bricks (red)
thinking about something grey (sky) in a white shirt, dirt under her nails and the shape of lavender
cleared of passion flowers, grass and nasturtiums (green) under such condition of atmosphere, painting

conceived of as a space between its frame and the surrounding picture of the world, flat in that sense
like distance in the look of the ridge before sky descends, the same thought in her mind as she walks
up the stairs (corner) defining the left half of the page, whose previous words may have been erased

11

lights turned off at the corners of buildings (dawn) when the boy walks in, looks for his mother still half asleep, that moment including seven birds on the bare branches of the tree, an overhead view of roofs (flat) in planes the color of sky whose blue and white doesn't want to be named, isn't

driving at night to the city, voices in the background where someone is asking the person (something) one forgets, who might otherwise be reading the play instead of acting in that part, cars on bridge whose lights move in a constant line, the man conscious of doing this (idea) thinking it not given

as vertical grey white band positioned right of center, which intersects (abstract) thought itself viewed on left branch, second bird (disappeared) landing in the other tree, a man identified by name who doesn't want to talk on the phone, the vertical (pale) red bar beside which darker strips of green

above blue (horizontal) something like a step, the third event in a series of significant objects
drawn on paper, diagonal white line coming into picture from lower right to upper middle (quadrant)
interrupting sleep in that sense, smell of hair on a pillow beside which he turns over, taken place

across the table speaking of paint on a board (diptych) in black and white squares, glasses (broken)
wanting to be seen in that light, the driver in a car caught in headlights leaving a crowded room
with person who isn't described, because she isn't in the picture (continuous) wrapped in a box

form of present duration, not being able to sleep (waking) at night, a pair of lenses on the table
(glass) where he leaves his watch, sound of clock returning to consciousness of the body wrapped
asleep under quilt, walking up steps to a door which opens (yellow) on left turned on its side

letter opened (illegible) to say she is moving, limpid suggesting not how much but often the body

turns over, feels what doesn't happen after months of not touching (experience) the other person,

not the man who talks on the phone after surgery (ravaged) whose skull will be drained of fluid

picture walking down the gutter, moss like algae after weeks of rain entering on the left (green)

which as he hits the concrete smashes (brain) consciousness on its side, no possibility of further

thinking in the sense that he hears the sound of his head cracking followed by the observer's voice

blue (unambiguous) transcribed as cerulean, brush strokes in the corner of an alien picture therefore

originally painted by a man whose name changes in the next scene, not the city with streets torn up

but expanse of field beyond barbed fence, lavender lifting its body as wind (colder) fingers back

14

from the north (east) blowing out mouth of lagoon, the man half-dressed thinking whether to go out

(water) or drive up hill to the house, whether he was dreaming or awake in that situation painted

as a series of rectangles parallel to the bottom of a picture (abstract) when turned on its side

not knowing which side is left, which "experience" the person at the table whose eyes are wet means

by the word "recognize," landscape viewed through condensation on a kitchen window in two dimensions

(vertical) extending from vines on a fence to the dark of ridge (line) below which water is in motion

"right" in red at the bottom of the frame, the second man's voice stronger (telephone) two days after

drilling a hole in his skull, pillow under the woman's hips lifting them upward (flat) from the bed

upon which the man is entering the picture (tongue), speaking of "dreaming in the pages of a book"

pulling grass shoots up from between the edges of two bricks (subject) equivalent in temporal form
to fluid being drained from the man's head, the woman who speaks of going on a journey to the desert
after which he will ask for her (anaesthetized) in a manner that will appear to suggest something else

feeling of a knife in his throat for example, her answer shifting from sound of water in the distance
(procedure) to the single heart-red tulip on the table around which children are standing, each one
about to describe the present moment (observed) meaning happens to be called, two pears on a sill

orange sliced in a white bowl (portrait) she returns to the kitchen, dialogue in the play wanting
to define the relationship between blue and the light blue shapes (geometric) thought to represent
each person's <u>former</u> self, conscious of how sky bisected by the white line the plane leaves appears

pattern of branches (crossed) outside the window, beyond which blue of overcast sky frames the second
person's arms, foreground imagined as a landscape of hand on shoulder in front of a window (exposed)
before she wakes up, walks into town with camera whose tender (orange) button appears to be stuck

girl holding the younger child in her arms, diagonal pink and blue lines left of center the hammock
under her (knees) eyes closed, color saturated at the edges of flowers whose centers can't be erased,
clouds whose motion reminds her of what it meant to be in that place, watercolor of glasses on a desk

limpid in that sense, an experience of that person's voice heard instead in the other person's ear
through which a feeling of loneliness can be displaced, the logic of such an image (fixed) involved
in walking across grass that's been cut, the green of it in clumps where the single brick is pressed

landscape framed in the open bedroom window (white) facing east, design imagined in series of receding

planes into which the viewer imagines himself placed (sound) waking with a fever, the second passage

repeated in a dream during the course of a night through which (surface) Orion continues to rotate

moonlight on his head when she falls asleep, canal meaning a "groove" appearing like a maze of lines

on the surface of a planet (Mars) viewed from Milan, this thought wrapped as if in a light blue gauze

whose atmosphere invites you to watch when the window blows shut, sounds of a shovel (outside) digging

woman in a white shirt under the rose, which catches when she moves close to the corner (exposed)

in that light, boy on the phone coming down with the same fever between the word and its sensation,

as if the subject itself could hear the scroll whose edge knocks against the stairwell, wind lifting bottom edge of the scroll (Chinese) like the landscape in the photograph of the man as a boy, angle of left hand on piano having played the same note for the listener, who hears the sound of a bird in the wind, fly on glass through which woman in blue starting to plant (poppies) in a painting

as owl glides across the page in two dimensions, less in focus the closer he looks (lens) on table, watercolor framed on the white wall in the upstairs room full of light (green) instead of the desk under window, what is outside the picture open to interpretation walking through a different house

painting on wall of lighthouse (imagined) opposite the stairs, the green car parked on the street where the girl's shoe (black) lies on its side in the gutter, left side of picture framed by green of distance which sound glides to in the shape of a crow (oblique) leaving its perch in the cypress other birds (smaller) perched on branches of plum beginning to leaf, vanished the moment he looks up

(reflection) left hand in window, glass bowl in which goldfish (magnified) continues to float below

consciousness, as someone who hasn't slept thinks of orange (horizon), house on a hill facing east

not falling asleep in that picture, bird with red breast on top right branch below which buildings

(white) may be seen, certain gestures in the play including the man who walks up to the car (locked)

the woman has left, significance of whose actions (offstage) the audience will only be able to guess

arrangement of buildings stacked on a hill, streets at oblique angle to impression of what it means

not to be sleeping, planes receding from left to right almost to the edge of blue (background) sky

above it, clock under the pillow that doesn't sound (theory) placed there by the woman beside him standing at the door in a brown coat about to leave (left) side of the picture, not wanting to sleep on the far side of the bed (reversed) turning her back on him, which takes place after conversation (diagonal) sitting across the table for four, the piano beside which someone plays a stand-up bass

green of bamboo out the window whose leaves are still wet, details of which translate to outward behavior of the body (evidence) when the man looks directly at her without speaking, such thinking whether the woman feels anything when the painting shows an interior world (abstract) as its subject

imagined as five tulips in the kitchen (still life) moving into the next room, whose temperature again becomes a topic of conversation between them, man on telephone talking to woman in building (understood) who listens to his description of such a place, the landscape instead of people in it condensation on the inside window through which sunlight (porous) passes on its way from cloudless

morning sky to person's eye (half-closed) thinking this, how his impression of the room implied

(parallel) by bands of color changes when he looks up, sees that the room itself isn't empty

woman sleeping in another room, which side of the bed depending on condition of observer (fever)

described in next scene, whose image keeps repeating itself as theme and variation in a color scale

(ridge) of green below sky blue, sound the only part of the picture perceived as birds in the distance

which explains "seeing" elsewhere, moon rising above ridge from perspective of water whose surface

lightens in the other direction as sun descends from top left to bottom right, dimension of tree

whose shape darkens without her seeing it (offstage) except to the extent that she imagines it

girl swinging on swing (dream) in nightgown, men at work in the streets below garden whose bricks
are seen only through weathered boards (foreground) of fence, this concept framed by waking in bed
to the sound of breath being pulled into chest, released (clouds) floating slightly off to the left

arm reaching over his shoulder, expanse of water to the left of the table (green) where the blue cup
represents a particular direction of thought, the girl on the telephone thinking (triangle) of yellow
at the bottom or left side of the picture whose plot includes the blue glass vase placed in the window

number multiplied by the third person on the phone (thought), who calls to explain what doesn't happen
(action) as knowledge of that experience might be performed in a play, boy actor playing the woman's
part as lines on paper (transcribed) wanting to meet him in another scene, opposite corner of room

23

(kitchen) she is cooking or otherwise engaged, man running in from across the yard repeated as image of the neighbor's house extended in space, appearance of light from an upstairs window (condensed) where the person sleeping calls out as if in the middle of her dream "if I mean something by it"

white building <u>not</u> present, a flat vertical column in its place a third of the way from the right side, man whose skull has been drilled to release build-up of fluids (hematoma) moving up the step to embrace him, woman beside him crossing the driveway (consequence) felt as the body moves against

shifting positions in the middle of the night, moon at diagonal (corner) window making it possible to see the man's action from above, how she turns her head to look up at <u>what is felt</u> by the object in a particular direction, sound transcribed as motion of blue shapes divided by angle of white line

24

angle of the sun at noon above a well (geometry) designed to calculate the earth's circumference,
slow-motion action of poppy opening between the time he first looks and a plane whose direction
is determined by its sound, waking in that position felt as the woman's hand reaches toward it

child's voice through the back door approximately close to the present moment, breath (exhaled)
heard in the distance as overtone scales wind conveys (northeast) swell dropping, which is after
the feeling an insect leaves on his left side prior to walking upstairs to bed, followed by a red

shadow of leaves on white wall (motion) opposite the man at the table, who turns toward the woman
on her side (right) facing away, how wind moves what otherwise isn't perceived except in passing
(accident) in that condition, the figure in the foreground understood as body moving its weight

blanket unfolded at the foot of the bed, the first person's legs pulled (back) as if by that gesture
meaning to have an 'experience' of meaning *here* (brushstroke) instead of the top left corner, wind
from northeast stronger than before that particular scene, connected by nuance of light and tone

yellow flowers (grass) in an orange vase on the table beginning to open, sunlight focused on next
thought in the window (interruption) climbing the face of water, wind blowing wave back over shape
"<u>what happened</u>" in the second frame (triptych) that morning, voice of the woman on a cellular phone

turning another direction (foreground), description of the watercolor improvised as an isolated case
of pink flower (edge), proportion of its body visible above the jade green surface of water ripped
open by wind's intensity, girl on couch not wanting something to change the walls of such a room

objects arranged as rhythm the line (mechanical) moves toward, man in dream viewed from left side leaning against wall (pattern) "between the picture and what it depicts," letters in that phrase visualized from above as knife on blue field, plate of shells on counter including coral (bone)

mother-of-pearl reduced to series of lines in a visual field (landscape) turned on its side, girl on sidewalk (seated) looking up at the man who isn't present, is therefore imagined as absence cuts across the face of the wave, the sun at that moment appearing to lift into the color that precedes it

whose last syllable is pronounced, elbows crossed on her knees in black and white (distance) focused as a shadow behind her to the left, the picture itself present as birds landing in tallest branches of still bare tree whose leaves (red) have begun to open, blue rectangular shape of cloth on table

two birds in the tree from above (sound) formed as the <u>possibility</u> of negation, what isn't present
walking out the door to the gate beyond which light appears inside the house, what she hears (hinge)
designated as length followed by curve of the back (participant) perceived as dark patches on screen

area opposite plane to this one, shadow transcribed as vertical white lines on a black field (grid)
beneath her, camera focused on a drop of blood on the sheet (angle) entering the film from the right
depending on the man's position, phenomenon of thinking this like waking up in the middle of the night

yellow flowers in an orange vase on the table, in front of which green of background (area) reflecting
motion of surface represented as water to left of blue car, two small figures in the distance placed
as if to describe what happens when the first person says "I have consciousness" in answer to that

brick turned on its side in tall grass, where the mower passes in front of the man facing (picture)
white wall on the opposite side of the bed, glasses on the windowsill next to the white hydrangea
(ground) below which two shapes intersect, one pair of legs raised to allow entrance of a second

landscape in frame standing on table, which faces the ridge at the far edge of a field (confusion)
below indifferent blue of field, grey white clouds and wash of what seems to be the sound of unseen
birds, smaller ridge at the edge of a wave about to break (color) white below green absence of ocean

light on surface (horizontal) represented as moving from the left, sound of gate where the woman walks
from a green car toward the person who hears it (reading) as absolute pitch, pink of the clouds above
shoulder after sunset fades (west) an assumption meaning the picture plays a part in all that's left

image of glass on the wall between doors, which is outside the stream of thought (being) present

the moment she answers the phone, person the father calls the next morning knowing she is awake

in the painting (unconscious) the first of whose figures appears to be thinking "I am dreaming"

feeling that way about such a person (intuitive) as kneeling down beside her in a form of thought,

object present in the sense that she can touch him or look at the picture a second time, watercolor

the daughter paints driving along the coast to meet someone (conjecture) under certain circumstances

motion of trees against a blue sky, white rose on the neighbor's wall not in focus at that distance

possibly literal, as a woman walking in from the left isn't expected (deviation), glimpse of bird

in a straight line (emphasis) as the man leans into a curve below which slate of current moving ochre in relation to light, the closer he gets to the object seen the less its parts appear focused

(interruption) as patches of water between two buildings, the painting laid out in pencil and pen

filled in with blocks of color (sienna) whose rhythms of light and dark and tone may be thought

parallel theory, walking into a landscape of squares and grids and regimented shapes (reaction)

after which he begins to see it, horizontal line of a building or depth of light on a far hill's

edge loosing itself in the background (<u>absence</u>) the person next to him calls a sublime calm green

figure of cloud approaching from the northwest (compare) equivalent to next picture, man on the left

looking at plane of water from one point of view imagined as light reflected on surfaces, triangle

expressed as distinction between <u>this</u> series of pictures and corner of sky, sense of cold before

water as particles of atmosphere moving <u>after</u> an event whose consequence isn't complete, description
of a hill facing the viewer whose sense of space is measured as <u>this</u> color produced by mixing green
and blue in a series of arbitrary statements, a girl walking in the gate who thinks she isn't seen

cross-hatch of lines (diagonal) analogous to slope of hill opposite table a patch of whose surface
is beginning to rust, area of grid at bottom right possibly cars on a roof parked in order of lines,
the pencil in the picture imagined as hand moving in front of the window (division) looking at night

other color of dress (orange) represented as close-up of leaves coming out on a branch where no bird
sings, the sound of wind in lavender bending it forward (unconscious) described as a hand gestures
at words whose emphasis isn't noticed, as if what happened fills the painting at just that point

shapes in plum branch leaving, whatever lingers in the present noticed as light on surface of water
the significance of which is concealed in black and white, viewer standing at the window who sees
triangle of white sail on blue water (field) at the same time a bird arrives in different sound

being transcribed as surface against surface, opaque in the sense its color is thought to appear
moving into that field in full view, ground on which the person who enters stops to ask a question
turning to the door which is outside what's visible (framed) in two dimensions, supposedly flattened

area between the appearance of roof lines (parallel) beyond whose substance other buildings happen
to be seen as an action determined not by eye but light of being in it, grey field above distant
hills understood as part of a particular scene (horizon) coming forward as the present subject

returning to light, color recurring as if behind the screen which is background to that conversation, figure on porch standing back to look at the man speaking of a series (example) of actions, profile of the woman pulling her arms to her chest according to lines in the picture, wind from northeast

flags on buildings against blue sky (saturated) when color takes the form of the person listening whether he can see or not, interpreted as a matter of logic beside the cat with a bird in its mouth walking across grid of bricks in the lower right hand corner, branches of tree with leaves coming out

photograph of boy looking up from bottom left, perception of which enters at sounds of cars in street below window, shape of the figure related to what the man is thinking reflected in transparent plane (glass) between him and the opposite hill, below which a bird lands and takes off in the foreground five pink petals visible to the right of the cypress above whose uppermost branches (green) white

clouds drifting, inside of which the yellow of the unnamed sexual part suggests an emotional effect

of the hand on paper (scrawl) moving to transcribe what the body feels waking up alone in its own bed

no sound but birds, the occasional car passing on the far side of a slatted fence perceived as second

of two actions (<u>internal</u>) compared to the woman walking downstairs to the phone not meaning to speak

in that blend of color positioned at right angle to person on the left, edge of wave about to break

theory of painting (color) *this* transition between two shapes on a hill and the white of foreground

flattened to suggest what the man sees looking up at it, not that he doesn't want to be seen exactly

like an object in a particular vision described in a series that starts with blue and ends with green greyish white streak of sky above ridge (horizontal) in middle of frame, which disappears when the man

turns on the light, thinking to _interpret_ the meaning of events previous to waking after not falling

asleep, purple of iris on table analogous to the fact that the woman is missing from chair on left

before which blank, sound of frogs in the field through plane of window perceived as a person turns

over upstairs (meaning) not knowing whether she intended to be separate, how it looked in conclusion

implied by the feeling in a different body instead of being able to sleep _under certain circumstances_

having absorbed the other person's color, sense of that gesture _here_ meaning "experience," impression

of woman focused on the substance of their conversation (invisible) whether a viewer notes its color

reflected in such light or not, an appearance beyond of shape described in this area of the picture divided by white (vertical) edge of the window frame, scene looking out to slope of ridge below white

clouds drifting, lighter blue above it perceived as third band of color in such a position (concept)

involved in what happens when that person walks into the room wanting to be seen and/or spoken to

memory of shape separated by angle of line, triangular blue patch on left standing for the woman

dressed like a man, reverse angle of forearm (abstract) reaching out to touch what the viewer sees

in the slope of her left shoulder, hair falling in the first of three performances of the same scene

pattern of landscape above which plane of sky (blue) which isn't color but light passing through it

from top right corner of painting itself, that series of events imagined in another tone of voice

as silence that follows when the woman falls asleep, rhythm of breathing proportionately slowed wavelength of sound (water) in series of pipes perceived as the temporal dimension, figure of the man

leaning back on a wall behind which sound elevates as bird lifting from the window disappears, grid

of horizontal blinds open on side of adjacent house whose occupant may or may not be moving about

woman in picture leaning on what appears to be the back of a metal chair (forearm) repeated as image

on left side of table, another picture of same person arranged in black and white field in the middle

of which a box of letters represents thought, a window half-closed onto grey light of the far-off edge

description like music, parallel slats in the floor extending to same wall viewed from another angle,

what is outside heard as the rhythm of colors and sound in a different time frame, memory of figure

lifting hand to his head between words (unconscious) as if anything in that place *could* be present

shifting perspective the second time (awake) impression of same sounds behind the wall, the body
in two dimensions appearing to lift its left arm (parenthetical) above shoulder, color interrupted
by the white of headlights as a car turns to face the viewer (interior) standing directly in its way

blue of painting remembered as man standing across (window) from her, woman moving her hand in time
to rhythm of words in the microphone inspired by his words, brushstroke in top corner significant
in the sense that shape coming into the room is reflected as light (field) in relation to glass

angle (exact) of body in relation to hers, close-up of face in blue and white afterimage of woman
being approached from behind, motion of man against her causing her to move (forward) as background
to what is happening elsewhere on the screen, first person identical except for color (blond) of hair

subtracted from image as color (line), activity of shapes moving opposite eye of the reader who fails

to explain their significance, private in that sense as objects the brush makes scraping away paint

in reference to what (thought) doesn't happen, light around the edges juxtaposed to figure's back

represented as subject (pictured) intersects the line between what one says and how she hears it

rotated from the left, that allusion to landscape from left (exterior) side of a window facing out

shifting to perspective of light source positioned on right side of body, detail of two women in bed

men leaning over the counter, isolation of the body in relation to close-up of head (torso) or chaos

of rocks on the windowsill viewed by the observer who sits in a car moving sideways in front of it,

composition in red (yellow) and/or blue whose structure pictures an aspect of the material world

direction of pink cloud as the picture rotates to the right (horizontal) from the man's perspective,
feeling of tension in the second person (shadow) interrupted when he speaks in another tone of voice
or comes downstairs in the dark, this shift of focus to the street (solitude) from that point of view

green of table beside two chairs (empty) also green, beyond which portion of the sky's glass changes
color in next scene, as if orange behind white or grey of cloud through glass were like description
(abstract) or description of leaves coming out on the branch equal to less than that which is seen

feeling of leg tucked under, arm across the shoulder of the person (sideways) after falling asleep
in that position or the next, depth of field from table to the woman standing in front of the window
the plane of whose back (vertical) faces it, dimension of light exterior to its presence on the branch

or lifting off the person in the first place, identification of shapes to the right of the brick path
(lavender) determined by color, purple of flower or violet in the span of a certain action repeated
as light, a line phrased in that system of thought (crossing) stopped at the bottom of the street

man at public phone calling for help, image of the woman at the top of the stairs prior to opening
bathrobe (pictured) on the couch below the window perpendicular to the figure slumped back in chair
(beige) opposite the front door, duration of that sequence measured by the distance between thoughts

weight of object itself (experience) on the viewer's right, appearance in the painting of details
perceived in eye's motion back to edge of next event, close-up of the wood floor from that position
above the shoulder (exposed) not described but thought equivalent to bird at flower, leaf on a branch

brick path on periphery of the viewer's world, whose momentum through it continues to leave behind

the experience of phenomena (abstract) moving toward the present, shadow of tree branch against grey

of sky which begins after sound of the song sparrow (independent) heard as if from the body's exterior

pink transposed from air above ridge to surface of rose petals one of which falls, the one previously

closed standing in a series of curves lit from below the horizon, parabola of sun before it appears

in the second of two planes (translucent) seen by the man who becomes at that moment a part of it

that figure minus a fraction of its slope against back (wall) the front of whose image is reversed,

the painting also similar to what it replaces (horizontal) observed from the same interior position,

feeling of correspondence evolved as a series of adjustments made to reflect what the man would feel

43

talked about afterward in another scene the man hears waking up, person at the house who reads <u>this</u> series of letters corresponding to <u>this different</u> situation, layers of pink clouds flattened against pale blue sky before what lights its surface becomes visible to the second person (expected) thinking

color of light in <u>alternative reading</u>, driving back across the bridge elsewhere in a separate action understood in order to be seen, his relation to that person as thought (philosophical) or the shape of a second hand in the mirror (transparency) painted as background, sun as it climbs behind cloud

woman across a table whose hair is pulled back (logic) choosing to be understood, whose position appears to change between "reddish green" and "yellowish blue" at a different angle (psychological) which isn't this, <u>this</u> concept approximately opposite the branches of a tree into which birds arrive

visible from the man's point of view, location described as a phenomena of objects on a table named
in terms of color, green of a candle or the purple of iris in a glass left from a previous person
who isn't present <u>here</u> except as gesture (nuance) taken to mean experience in a different light

triangular wedge in lower right corner (abstract) not purple, which continues yellow of foreground
below a series of vertical blue planes conceived of as the impression of color, smell of older woman
who leans across the space of a room prior to exit (point) saturated as green of adjacent room's walls

calculation of the depth of that painting's field a matter of literal significance, <u>this</u> way of seeing
multiple surfaces in three dimensions (flat) analysis of which begins at the right edge of the frame,
"sameness" in ratio of white to light grey to black (opaque) thought to make sense of actual color

sound of the man's voice ascending a passage (imagined) after which he sees petal fall from a rose
in a vase on the table, its whitish pink not in itself a negative proposition of grey (white) sky,
alternative sound of birds calling back and forth between an unseen place and perceiving subject

interior projection of surface (ground) whose slope appears to be measured by an instrument placed
at a certain distance from that point, as if water moving across it falls in that direction (gravity)
away from the window, two small patches within this area turning as it happens a darker shade of green

a second rose beginning to open next to it, its scent filling the doorway between where it appeared
at the edge of the yard and its position in front of the painting, horizontal suggestions of green
(foreground) water to the left of a series of cross-hatched lines which represent streets on hill

distinction between an image of rose in a glass and the subject itself, weight of pink flower (trace) bending its stem to the left within the field of what is present, view of third person at the table (transparency) through the window to the green of ridge not obscured by grey white being of clouds

illumination from behind which isn't visible, an object having left the room exactly as it appears (translation) in terms of the role of logic in color represented as light, bricks in the foreground experienced as sounds falling in a musical phrase (birds) the significance of which isn't understood

concealment of lines in a picture whose color follows it, nuance of green after rain in the distance more like shadow on a surface than anything blue (concept) compared to black and white, phenomenon of image distinguished from what is seen *here* as mental picture 'saturated' with sound and light panorama of grey scale on two sides of a corner (window) beyond which the invisible world, rotation

of which concept may be described in the sound of cars in the street or the woman in a green robe

whose molecular structure moves through a transposition of shadows (psychological) out the door

light in a state of perpetual vibration an <u>imaginable answer</u>, "X" in another sense the darker blue

feeling of sky the <u>essence</u> of which is proposed behind cloud (relationship) in that light, analysis

of shape similar to branches at the top of a tree which doesn't produce color but rather receives it

the person waking up expressed as an analogy to thought itself (condition) looking out through glass,

duration of a specific tone measured as pitch is said to *leave* the body whose weight is non-spatial

in other words, this experience of the flower on her left (spectrum) corresponding to feeling <u>this</u>

way of seeing ridge (intersection) below the now pale blue area of sky above it, view of the window
previously remembered on a plane (geometrical) moving away from the man's present position toward
this thing, light coming into it at lower (first) left pane of window meaning the sun is rising

anticipation of being in that physical place (opaque) including the bed, depth of visual field
(direction) in which three birds disappear to the left of color followed by two others, this way
of analysis recalling the grey black wall behind the woman whose reading (background) doesn't stop

grid of a map between one series of moments and the previous one (appended) as though concluding
were sometimes possible, sound of bird's wings before looking up to see it isn't action (heard)
along the curve of its flight, field (horizontal) out of which sensation of other sound stops

before that (particular) bird appears, action in the picture focused on the second of two figures
walking into the present scene (outside) which isn't black and white, speaking of her experience
of the green and yellow surfaces of water or darker (memory) green shape of the ridge beyond it

vertical edge of window (closed) which shuts out thought of sound, person knee-deep at the edge
(motion) of primarily white water looking as the man walks up the beach, an arrival at this place
of transition lingering as <u>this</u> presence (scene) continues in the transparent light that follows it

look of back from behind it (exposed) as action, how the color of her hair falls across it depending
on the position of the observer (participant) <u>concept</u> of which enters from the right, <u>this picture</u>
related to what actually happened as description of something <u>behind</u> glass means to interpret it

expanse of greyish white sky before dawn (continued) shifts the relation of objects within it, edge
of man's leg folded over her after talking in the dark (series) elsewhere, the action of the woman
driving through the fence illuminated as surface whose <u>lightest</u> color appears to leave it changed

feeling of grids (abstract) analogous to birds disappearing into the same tree, angle of branches
<u>different</u> in the order of fragments named as a sequence of four colors, red less than blue or white
more than the idea of the flower below the window (mechanical) instead of thinking she is leaving him

area between the observer and <u>this</u> thought conceived as something else, second figure opposed to flat
shape of buildings to the northwest in an aerial view (geometric) below color and weight of clouds,
the meaning of not being in this place with this person discovered after the fact of such events

yellow of Scotch broom arranged in a brown field (horizontal) perceived from upstairs point of view

having turned the body over to approach it from behind, position <u>vis-à-vis</u> the blue white (presence)

of two birds moving across the bedroom window visualized as transparent places in the field beyond it

entering <u>this picture (diminished)</u> as effect of sound or color "saturated" with sense, that feeling

sometimes expressed through glass or the weight of the body (theory) moving under it, what happens

then concealed as if to linger further (thing) in the physical relation of front to back surfaces

material becoming a black and white event, curve of shape reversed as the image rotates to the left

(foreground) in retrospect, the difference between being together as a <u>process</u> of colors painted out

and the "finished" picture of what takes place (impression) <u>because</u> of that analogy to object as fact slope of surface determined by direction of water flowing toward or away from the man standing on it

thinking it is <u>going</u> to happen <u>this</u> way, shape of bird passing overhead in grey of sky before dawn

a phenomenon of color in the painting perceived (continuous) as variation of colors in the field

outside <u>expression</u> of this, increase of light (compare) meaning it will be possible to describe <u>what</u>

someone could see looking out the window of an upstairs room, projection of birds in green and yellow

foreground beyond which a darker green abstraction of trees (concept) whose sound is only now arriving

interrupted by the edge between two people and what produces it, the man having climbed up the cliff

before being in the semi-grey of water (sometimes) compared to the woman standing at the edge of it

seen from that position, a <u>certain</u> blue of iris in her hand (yellowish) "mixing" in relative light

improbable as man's body next to the bed climbing into it (analogy) on top of the other, glimpse
of content between <u>one</u> sound (<u>internal</u>) and the slightly different one that follows it <u>for example</u>
when he lifts up his arms, asks the listener to visualize an image of rope breaking strand by strand

something crossed out, which erases the surface of this picture compared to its feeling (intention)
the actual body as it wraps itself around <u>Woman in a Red Blouse</u> in three dimensions, visual space
(transparent) surrounding the object whose form is experienced from many angles at the same time

continuation of <u>that</u> phenomenon being peculiar to someone else, as looking up from above the tree
into whose branches birds have arrived isn't action but present thought, <u>how the composer intended</u>
someone else to be interrupted by the sound of the man holding his breath (appearance) releasing it

below plane of grey white sky (visual) beyond which a part of the conversation registers as shape

of trees on distant ridge, which elsewhere approaches the system of thought (position) <u>interpreted</u>

between the body's diagonal motion across a surface (wave) and the green translucent glass it rides

expanse of ocean compared to its depth (space) walking up hill to the left, that feeling registered

as small blue elements in a field composed of cross-hatched lines (iris) whose <u>alternative picture</u>

may include the figure asleep on a bed (therefore) without waking to whatever lingers next awhile

line of the building curved from lower left to middle third of background, two figures (luminous)

one of whom is listening to the <u>phenomena</u> of silence the other brings from left of painting itself,

as if the viewer who looks into her mind <u>means to want that</u> particular circumstance rather than this sense of the arrangement of words on a page <u>intended by the composer</u> in relation to their sound

(picture) sung by multiple voices, "white" for example overlapping "black" or "blue" on "green"

whose <u>essence</u> is indecipherable to the listener (thought) for whom something else takes place

sound then of birds (invisible) in the field below the upstairs window, what someone sees of color

<u>recognized</u> as the grey-white layer of fog that moved in the night prior to that view, this action

being present as a horizontal band above the frame (imagined) which becomes the landscape itself

picture on wall to the left of the window of the person who calls from somewhere else, sky light

(overcast) where blue in another dimension would be darker above her and the man she is touching,

position of her right hand draped over his left shoulder perceived as two or more separate events orange of first of three poppies in a vase (thought) around the yellow center, <u>that</u> color similar

to the concept of someone else's body moving across an adjacent room (etc.) in transition from red

to yellow <u>or</u> green, condensation on the window through which sound of birds in the field isn't seen

departure of the green car into <u>present</u> being, woman behind the wheel an allusion to "N" (picture)

feeling this description of visual phenomena, irregular line of ridge (horizontal) between the blue

white of sky and its own spectrum of color predicted by the sum of that experience driving toward it

theory of painting what happened to <u>him, this</u> gesture taking place as a "mental activity" for example

<u>subsequently thinking</u> the temperature outside is slightly cooler than <u>"I" want in a different sense</u>

(interpreted) to feel it, waking in the foreground to a diagonal view of her head on his shoulder random motion of branches in the space between viewer and shadows on ridge before light (continued)

whose action is also part of color, what it means to the person at the window thinking <u>this must be</u>

the "solution" of pure color (<u>marginal</u>) as a bird crossing over the field appears to move through it

sound through glass <u>not</u> amplified, which becomes an emotional <u>effect</u> for the woman kneeling in front

of the bench (position) to whom <u>nothing is said</u>, the <u>possibility</u> of objects on the table taken away

analogous to <u>what</u> she appears to be doing there replaced by the sound of the cat wanting to get in

diagonal field of light to left of middle frame (center) the <u>understanding</u> of which is complicated

by <u>effects</u> of wind (northwest) on the color of water below it, what happens when she opens the door

<u>beginning the sentence</u> more slowly than the feeling (opposite) that something is surrounded by light

color below edge of ridge before it rises (irregular) toward the person driving in someone else's car (green) around the lagoon toward it, condition of the child under the freeway at the same time <u>found</u> to be a physical presence (verified) coming back to the prior position of the black and white house

activity of other <u>possible</u> birds measured as sound (invisible) in the first place, shape of the body bent over shovel at ground level (psychological) whose surface slopes away from corner of building, concept (<u>ambiguous</u>) between a diagonal white line and feeling of man standing in opposite corner

stones being moved by hand in slow motion (experience) a geometry of color, the way sound of another bird enters the window more insistently once it is opened by <u>someone else in the same way</u>, hearing it in the foreground (frame) from whose absence of water a deeper tone appears to be rising through green image of bed outside in the rain (underline)painting(/underline)) when the man opens the door followed by action of woman

(background) as transparency of surface related to prior color, the way pink will come into clouds

before the sun itself appears (expected) accompanied in a particular area by sound of first birds

triangle of pale green in middle left experienced as the color of wave from water level, someone else

facing the viewer from behind the concept of sounds ("luminous") occurring in a different dimension,

pure yellow turning to consciousness at the center of phenomena which isn't present in that sense

grey of clouds a visual 'picture' of alternative thought (action) to man on telephone hanging up,

three-dimensional body of the person on the white surface of a bed being lighter than yellow here

(logic) described as the content of a subject comparable to evidence of the color one doesn't know configuration of objects on the table projected by means of sighting along parallel lines (concept)

as opposed to the blue or yellow curve of <u>anything</u> abstract, formal shape made possible by naming

background "Indian Red" (translation) shadows which show that light is coming from offstage left

that sensation <u>described</u> by a horizontal line through the middle of the window beyond which <u>nothing</u>

appears, outline of shaped branches of a tree where the sun comes up coincident to drops of water

on the edge of leaves (impression) and the <u>rendering</u> of an auditory system in a secondary sense

spectrum moving from yellow to blue depending on viewer's perspective, which is <u>how</u> someone 'sees'

the relation between events from the outside (ambiguous) as the surface <u>colors</u> of a visual field,

blue of iris on green of its stem an approximate description when viewer looks up from the left

thinking of colors in an immediate sense (chemical) instead of the body next to the woman in bed,
flat of shoulder in that light resting under the downward pull of the other hand (detail) <u>function</u>
whose gesture is felt in detail, idea of surface in contrast to something moving from yellow to blue

shape of a body moving across the upper left quadrant of picture after its sound (recognized) behind
which circumstances something actual <u>isn't</u> thought, person's right arm for example between the door
and nearly vertical slope of rock (geometry) adjacent to content, blue of sky as physical presence

<u>experience</u> of light coming out of space as something enclosed between 'feeling' of voluntary motion
and <u>this</u> memory of an arm gone to sleep, how presence of bird (fragment) happens by accident outside
the window designated by the sound it articulates approaching and passing through the middle distance

view above field toward plane of ridge still in shade (gesture) bisected by vertical frame of window either open or <u>somewhat</u> closed (distinction) depending on idea of wind moving across it, perception of white hydrangea in a vase <u>rarely</u> observed as direct action changed by (gradual) motion of light

moments of afterimage apparent as glass (recognized) which moves behind a wall understood as <u>logical</u> thought of person leaving in a car, drops placed in the eye of the beholder therefore a psychological action with respect to the green of leaves draped over glass or lifting on the branch still outside it

yellow <u>selected</u> from the possible spectrum of <u>some</u> colors, meaning how the second person <u>isn't</u> present to the left of the white column (abstract) within whose space a pair of triangular blue fields appear coincident with that fact, the illusion of one's absence an "optical mixture" of yellow next to blue name of color standing for the object or person implied as a concept which produces light or the blue

(approximate) it moves across from one situation to the next, disjunction of bodies in the same room

represented as a series of "pure" colors the <u>importance</u> of which can't be described to someone else

exactly what happens between such events, the woman's feelings for example subject to active movement

possibly after the man returns (<u>logical</u>) subdivided into innumerable tones, call of the song sparrow

at first light in combination with his hand and the shoulder it follows (voluntarily) thinking that

plane of field surrounded by thought (horizontal) as <u>this experience</u> of light or <u>this</u> one, transparent

body of evidence taken as a visible impression the meaning of whose effects (substitute) confused her,

diagram of green "saturated" to the extent that one looks beyond it to an interval of opposing color approximate grey of buildings <u>surrounding</u> the emotion of that experience as an acoustic interval comparable to light, how the man wakes in the middle of the night (<u>intention</u>) for the same reason that someone moving in a parallel relationship to objects could also see yellow brighter than blue

how light comes into the room compared to its sound, the figure at the left edge of this proposition (diagram) overlapped by her darker resemblance to someone whose angle <u>might</u> appear as a more exact "psychological" <u>expression</u> adjacent to the visible portion of the body intersected by its effect

analysis of blue glass in whitish light <u>complicated</u> by her feeling in relation to the middle distance, <u>that</u> geometry of the senses made more certain by the gradual appearance of interior lines (rectangle) whose surface <u>can't</u> be connected to what happened in a film of color between one shape and the next presence of a bird landing in same tree <u>now</u> (pattern) or leaving, as if the physics of its behavior could be described by thinking of the same event in both of its different appearances (perceptible) "pulling" away from each other in the following situation <u>one</u> of whose actions will be indistinct

color of body <u>seen</u> in the reflection of shoulder in window connected in <u>that</u> two-dimensional plane to further uncertainty, the blue light of <u>cloudiness</u> articulated as a multiplicity of flat shapes <u>over there</u> (distant) which isn't only specific to the placement of the middle color on the floor

concept of <u>space</u> therefore <u>philosophical</u>, investigation of which continues as "thinking" of color through the white surface of glass either by moving <u>beyond</u> it (transparent) or looking horizontally at a figure "equidistant" between an arrangement of blue and yellow and the experience of its absence reverse view from above understood as conscious thought of what it means when the man calls at night in that particular case or (b) the simplicity of evidence apparent when the feeling of that person intersects that of the second as a physical dispersion of sunlight overlapping a mixture of grey

shape of buildings in the following diagram standing for exterior action, someone else's statement approaching a wedge of faded green to the left of the piano (visual) imagined to be what the girl whose cropped head is playing it hears connected to the physical presence of color in that plane

the absence of that person's psychology in the picture overlapping its logical opposite (observed) as if one could see "red" in the interior expression of such thought under certain circumstances, grey of buildings subtracted from the illusion that one sees a specific example of that subject

vibration of color refracted against the real (instinct) phenomena of seeing, before which meaning
both the physical presence of an object "in-between" yellow on top of green (surface) and content
described in its place are recognized as one logic of appearances in relation to possible others

"thought-out" system of overlapping planes drawn by hand in two dimensions parallel to the bottom
edge of blue, transparency of ochre or the pink of poppy (curve) to the left of five other similar
shapes part of a rhythm determined by placing that imagined concept of color next to feeling itself

feeling of the afterimage simultaneous to what happens when a person first walks into the room, not
independent of that experience of a body at the edge of a circle of seeing but blue green contrast
instead of white in it (position) complementary to an illusion of a different physiological shape

"reflective" geometry of light against the vertical planes of buildings seen from above (calculation) expressed as grey white feeling of color, subtraction of a body moving across the sky at <u>that</u> angle before the presence of the spectrum changes to <u>what</u> someone <u>sees</u> in such motion of shapes on water

appearance of the man in the opposite direction first (semi-darkness) parallel to the relationship between "black" and "red," which leads in a similar experiment to <u>real</u> objects absorbed in <u>thinking</u> the concept of "opposing" (complementary) colors applied to the feeling of lighter and darker ground

psychology of <u>these exact</u> shades like "behavior" of the woman in the middle of the room, this color (diagram) together with pieces of blue sky placed according to the 'sameness' of physical surfaces whose architecture <u>means</u> to be viewed from his position (brightness) as a three-dimensional shape

69

arrangement in the foreground of light and darker <u>places not somewhere</u>, intensity of visual effect
(abstract) shifting back and forth between the sound of the second person's <u>sensation</u> of "feeling"
two diagonal lines in empty space (body) and the analogy of a different gesture in place of that

wind from the northwest registered as perception of branches (sound) in trees, "X" pointing to action
in the middle of a film as a verbal expression of the same <u>theory</u> (A) presentation of which remains
"colorless" in the sense that a person's behavior reflects the logic of primary "yellow" or "grey"

other sound divided into opaque colors, white observed as part of the phenomenon of the man's face
seen <u>via</u> its previous appearance in flattened light (reproduction) exaggerated by surrounding areas
of color (example) the character of whose relationship changes at the lower left edge of the picture

smooth white surface of a plane against which viewer imagines building (series) <u>this</u> building, the way a bird's sound <u>appears</u> in a white room corresponding to something in a <u>different</u> experience of "white" (transparent) the intensity of whose afterimage was <u>seen</u> in a pattern of <u>being</u> in two places at once

overlapping of possible tones at intervals recognized for example as a "colorless" <u>impression of white</u> (mechanical) parallel to 'thought' of it, the pink of a rose at the corner of the window <u>now</u> visible distinguished by the logic of its physics (proposition) by what it <u>really</u> looks like in that light

simultaneous effect of straight lines (pencil) suddenly intimate, <u>how</u> what happens as an arrangement of parts in a pattern <u>like this</u> means 'something' consequently different from the fact of its shape and/or size on paper under analogous conditions (temperature) multiplied by that <u>mathematical rule</u>

behind the same color (psychological) images of a particular object something appears to look like,
green moving away from the center of the picture whose left edge is described by one sound perceived
in front of its opposite ('transparent') prior to blue of sky above it through which other sounds move

trajectory of line following the sound of its name ("white") which forces the mind to follow the story
of the image as verbal picture, how that expression of light dissolves in two-dimensional atmosphere
"read" as a pairing of tone with color (unconscious) where the edge of something yellow turns blue

actual "situation" of blue white band of clouds (horizontal) above line of ridge, thought about it
happening in two directions at once (triangle) as if painting becomes the feeling of a certain area
of the painting imagined (theory) as an obscure color equal to 'color' of trees going on without end

sound (system) "tuned" to register the far away color of ocean at the end of the road, blue white instead of the green between blue and yellow plane of field to the right of two figures (hesitation) "shape" articulated as a series of parallel lines whose subsequent interaction is therefore continued

"green" repeated as the sound of a bird projected across presumably flat <u>note</u> of intermediary plane (pigment) as the fact of this anatomical "picture" relates to reading what happens between colors, <u>like an appearance</u> of yellow green or blue green <u>deviation</u> from which has nothing to do with it

glimpse of more distant cloud <u>not</u> physical (example) continued as a sense of detail between tones, position of "X" in a certain light following the description of a wave (length) which doesn't exist except in two dimensions <u>he</u> says (note) thinking of the relationship between certain "primary" colors factual "size" of an object relative to internal appearance in contrast to the color of its surface, "what actually happened" remembered as a visual phenomenon whose effect is related to that "action" someone else calls <u>pure yellow</u> ("iridescent") as an analysis of its auditory perception concludes

color of bird on the opposite branch <u>expected to be brown</u> in that position, which sound continues in relation to the length of the smaller of two objects in <u>this</u> "series" (comparison) whose system of logic isn't continuous but <u>prior</u> to "green" (transparent) as the color of that word will suggest

pattern in the field of green beside yellow therefore "psychological," figure in lower left corner approaching the triangular blue wedge above it (<u>ambiguous</u>) in addition to the effect of its color between areas in a two-dimensional field punctuated by sound (sequence) of second bird on branch figure at piano in semi-darkness (anaesthetized) moving fingers in <u>this</u> or <u>that</u> pattern of sound, the color of light in relation to its 'meaning' in two or three dimensions (opaque) given the same visible action subdivided in the following diagram into surfaces or <u>conscious effect</u> and its reverse

color of <u>this</u> white wall a physical fact (angle) whose psychological effect depends on the difference between "yellow" and "green," as someone who <u>thinks this concept must be different</u> "feels" its color decreased or gradually added (translation) to this volume of blue green in proportion to its "depth"

<u>what</u> happens next in the middle distance (southeast) to <u>these</u> dark shades of trees whose surfaces haven't yet arrived in light, hand on white ground of table describing an <u>important</u> fact (geometric) of lines a bird makes descending from upper left corner to the empty space immediately in front of it

horizontal "complex" of palest reds above where ridge bisects white of window frame, point of <u>this</u> <u>given</u> sound like "feeling" the presence of space between the woman's perspective (blue) and the way something in the arrangement of vertical planes in a building <u>contains</u> another "reading" of its form

reflection of hand on paper in the window <u>marginal</u> to experience of "white" reversed in <u>not white</u>, someone closing the door arriving by analogy in a shapeless room the meaning whose system of colors (relationship) can be taken as arbitrary evidence of the angle from which sunlight might come into it

<u>this</u> physical example (background) instead of the sound of unseen birds from tree or green of field extending below it, the person walking out the door who won't be seen as "difference of substance" continuous with <u>impression</u> of white cloud <u>behind</u> blue of sky (translucent) changed by that fact

one color placed on top of the next in a two-dimensional plane whether <u>this fact</u> "has color" or not,
the person facing the wall against which light is "reflected" from a position behind him to the left
who will experience <u>this</u> phenomenon between "blue and red" (lines) which aren't in that event audible

something <u>important</u> crossed out (confusion) between related areas of darker and <u>light red for example</u>,
what that means depicted as the weight or volume of someone's <u>real behavior</u> seen from the direction
light is passing through, what "music" <u>can do</u> as an accompaniment to thought of a "luminous white"

shape the <u>same</u> as "precise" bluish mixture of sky with semi-dark green (sometimes) planes below it,
<u>direction</u> of what appears to be a present moment of lighter blue "similar" to the feeling of a cloud
<u>designated</u> by less <u>certain</u> "primary color" (refined) characterized by the relative lightness of yellow

surface color of bricks <u>essentially this</u> "red," the figure of (someone) who thinks to walk across it

between <u>this object</u> (translucent) and the same <u>kind</u> of feeling named by innumerable shades of green

or the indefiniteness of a blue above it (weight) consequently changed in the "cast" of that light

someone crossing an imaginable "stage" reduced in proportion to distance from the same white wall,

grey white image of water (space) <u>not</u> blue after the concept of ochre in <u>this kind</u> of "performance"

of building on a hill facing the "actor" (intention) who appears to be <u>marginal</u> in a parallel sense

asymmetrical emphasis of "something white" above opposite <u>white</u> third of a different frame (relative)

which isn't an extension of its area, suggestions of other transparent colors analogous to the line

between quantities of green (dissonance) and the physics of that blue and/or violet surrounding it placement of this afterimage in a sequence of related events <u>before white, clouds</u> in changing light

described as perception of grey or white <u>color</u> ("vertical") moving from left to right at intervals

behind glass ("transparent") in whose reflection they will appear as auditory and/or optical fact

<u>same</u> indeterminate color <u>not supposed</u> to be the same, <u>another</u> purple of iris opening on the table

beyond which the receding planes of buildings on the opposite hill (arbitrary) <u>like</u> an alternative

reading of many-sided tones (acoustic) in relation to the <u>fifth</u> color to the right of next painting

vertical column of <u>pale</u> yellow to the left of blue and <u>lightest</u> blue (etc.) different from the space

in front of it, the separate effect of volume when opposing colors disappear in a sample of <u>reddish</u>

white tones (psychological) which is <u>what happens now vis-à-vis this</u> system of simultaneous sounds

bending-over head of pale pink rose (horizontal) in orange vase on table later saturated with light,
this description of "all that happens" connected to feeling of overlapping amounts of middle color
(diminished) beside the white that will sometimes disappear farther back in that prescribed space

simultaneous sounds of thinking, definition of this effect perceived through glass ("incomplete")
gradually reversed in the sequence of psychological gestures a person makes in response to "yellow"
or "bluish white" pattern (transparency) as an empirical fact of this physical experience before that

sudden impression of the same bird (sound) beyond left edge of window, which is always called "white"
adjacent to the emotional effect of pleasure (continuation) like "green" surrounded by light "grey"
or "white" seen in a parallel series of 1 + 1 + 1 transcribed in the next example as middle "red"

arrangement on the windowsill of grey and white edges of rocks (definition) beyond which "phenomenon" <u>impression</u> of grey white distance, the face of the person in another room placed to left of viewer at a <u>different</u> angle (series) corresponding to what <u>now looks white</u> instead of "grey" and "white"

bird on a branch transferred to a higher key (continuation) <u>only after this, foundation</u> understood as diagonal pairs of lines moving across a "yellow" or "grey" surface (diagram) or series of leaves on another branch related to the difference between <u>such</u> a picture (topographic) and what it depicts

"white" adjacent to "green" (<u>outside</u>) area involved with someone standing next to it, whose motion into semi-darkness is <u>not</u> an "optical" effect but <u>how what happens before one</u> feels "transparent" (something) or spatial <u>sense</u> of a perception "pushing" from yellow and blue to green by itself

81

gradual sameness of pink or grey or whitish <u>paint, how space</u> can be divided into "luminous" tones
either by moving the object away from its visual surface or placing it <u>over there</u> (lighter) <u>beyond</u>
"thinking" that something opaque can be "equidistant" from the second person's actual line of sight

color of green field (example) called "F" <u>there, this</u> surface of a table <u>roughly</u> described as brown
in comparison to the grey white possibilities of distance which appear above or below it (example)
between whose logic of three-dimensional planes <u>this</u> "cobalt blue" imagines something "and so on"

<u>exact</u> action "here" of "grey green" field observed in the second proposition like <u>thought about it,</u>
<u>the way</u> "I see" surrounded by additional amounts of blue and yellow (ochre) equally present at <u>this</u>
distance as "X" reversed in a following diagram (etc.) described by someone pointing to <u>what just is</u>

2.4.97 — 4.21.97

About the Author

Stephen Ratcliffe's most recent books are *Selected Days, CLOUD / RIDGE, Conversation, REAL* and *Portraits & Repetition*. His ongoing series of four 1,000-page books of poetry each written in 1,000 consecutive days is available at Editions Eclipse http://eclipsearchive.org/editions.html. He is also the author of three books of criticism, *Reading the Unseen: (Offstage) Hamlet, Listening to Reading*, and *Campion: On Song*. He lives in Bolinas, California and teaches at Mills College in Oakland.

About Chax Press

Chax Press is a 501(c)(3) nonprofit organization, founded in 1984, and has published more than 150 books, including fine art and trade editions of literature and book arts works.

For more information, please see our web site at http://chax.org

Chax Press is supported by individual contributions, and by the Tucson Pima Art Council and the Arizona Commision on the Arts, with funds from the State of Arizona and the National Endowment for the Arts.

TUCSON PIMA
ARTS
COUNCIL

Arizona
Commission
on the Arts

NATIONAL
ENDOWMENT
FOR THE ARTS